D1288349

Jackie ROBINSON

Breaking the Color Barrier

Sean Price

Chicago, Illinois

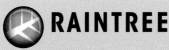
RAINTREE

TO ORDER:
☎ Phone Customer Service **888-454-2279**
💻 Visit **www.heinemannraintree.com** to browse our catalog and order online.

Editorial: Adam Miller
Design: Ryan Frieson, Kimberly R. Miracle, and Betsy Wernert
Photo Research: Tracy Cummins
Production: Victoria Fitzgerald

Originated by DOT Gradations Ltd
Printed and bound by Leo Paper Group

ISBN-13: 978-1-4109-3115-3 (hc)
ISBN-10: 1-4109-3115-3 (hc)
ISBN-13: 978-1-4109-3124-5 (pb)
ISBN-10: 1-4109-3124-2 (pb)

13 12 11 10 09
10 9 8 7 6 5 4 3 2 1

Library of Congress Cataloging-in-Publication Data
Price, Sean.
    Jackie Robinson : breaking the color barrier / Sean Price.
        p. cm. -- (American history through primary sources)
    Includes bibliographical references and index.
    ISBN 978-1-4109-3115-3 (hc) -- ISBN 978-1-4109-3124-5 (pb) 1. Robinson, Jackie, 1919-1972--Juvenile literature. 2. Baseball players--United States--Biography--Juvenile literature. 3. African American baseball players--Biography--Juvenile literature. 4. Discrimination in sports--United States--Juvenile literature. I. Title.
    GV865.R6P75 2008
    796.357092--dc22
    [B]
                    2008011296

Acknowledgments
The author and publisher are grateful to the following for permission to reproduced copyright material: ©AP Photo **pp. 18** (Marty Lederhandler), **27** (Jim Wells), **29** (Doug Kanter); ©Associated Press **pp. 7, 9, 20**; ©Corbis/Bettmann **pp. 5, 21, 23, 26, 12** (David J. & Janice L. Frent Collection), **28** (epa/John G. Mabanglo; ©Getty Images/Hulton Archive **p. 6**; ©Library of Congress Prints and Photograph Division **pp. 10, 15, 22**; ©Library of Congress Motion Picture, Broadcasting and Recorded Sound Division **p. 19**; ©National Baseball Hall of Fame Library Copperstown, N.Y. **pp. 4, 8, 11, 13, 14, 16, 17, 24B, 24M, 24T, 25B, 25T.**

Cover image of Jackie Robinson with the Montreal Dodgers used with permission of ©National Baseball Hall of Fame Library Coopperstown, N.Y.

The publishers would like to thank Nancy Harris for her assistance in the preparation of this book.

Contents

Some words are printed in bold, **like this**. You can find out what they mean on page 30.

Jim Crow Baseball

Baseball is sometimes called "America's game." It started in the 1800s. But back then, black Americans could not play with whites. They had to play on separate teams.

The Major Leagues had the best baseball teams. But these teams allowed only white players. That changed briefly in the 1880s. Moses Fleetwood Walker became the first black person to play in the Major Leagues. But white players did not like this. By 1887, Major League teams refused to hire blacks anymore.

Black people were kept out of the Major Leagues until 1947. That is when a brave black ballplayer put a stop to it. His name was Jackie Robinson.

Moses Fleetwood Walker's nickname was "Fleet."

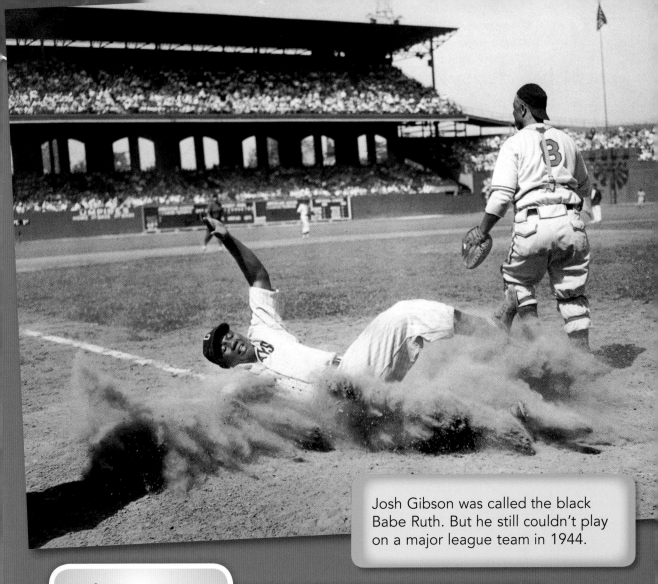

Josh Gibson was called the black Babe Ruth. But he still couldn't play on a major league team in 1944.

Jim Crow

In the 1800s, many whites did not believe black people were as good as other people. In the South, states passed **Jim Crow laws**. Jim Crow was the name of a black character in popular plays. Jim Crow laws **segregated** (separated) blacks from whites. Blacks went to separate schools. They even used separate bathrooms.

Jackie Robinson, All-Star

Jackie Robinson was born on January 31, 1919. He was born in Georgia, which is a southern state. His family was poor. Jackie was the youngest of five children.

Jackie's father left home when he was a baby. Jackie's mom moved the family to Pasadena, a city in California. She moved there to get a better job. Georgia had **Jim Crow laws**. California did not.

But some whites still bothered Jackie's family. They did not like blacks. They tried to force Jackie's family to move to a different area. Jackie's mother refused to leave.

This is Jackie Robinson with his family. He is the little boy wearing a hat.

Jackie Robinson practices for the UCLA football team.

Jackie got into trouble as a kid. He stole things from stores. The police watched him closely. Family and friends talked him into staying out of trouble. Soon he became a strong athlete. Jackie was asked to go to college at the University of California at Los Angeles (UCLA). He played many sports. He played track, football, basketball, and baseball.

Trouble in the army

Jackie wanted to become a **pro athlete**. That meant he would get paid to play sports. But his goal was delayed by World War II. The United States entered World War II in 1941. The army began a **draft**. That meant young men were told they must serve in the army. Jackie was drafted.

Jackie planned to become an army **officer**. That meant he would lead other men. But the army did not want black officers. Army leaders did not want blacks to be in charge of whites. Jackie fought against this. Finally, he became an officer.

Jackie Robinson in his army uniform.

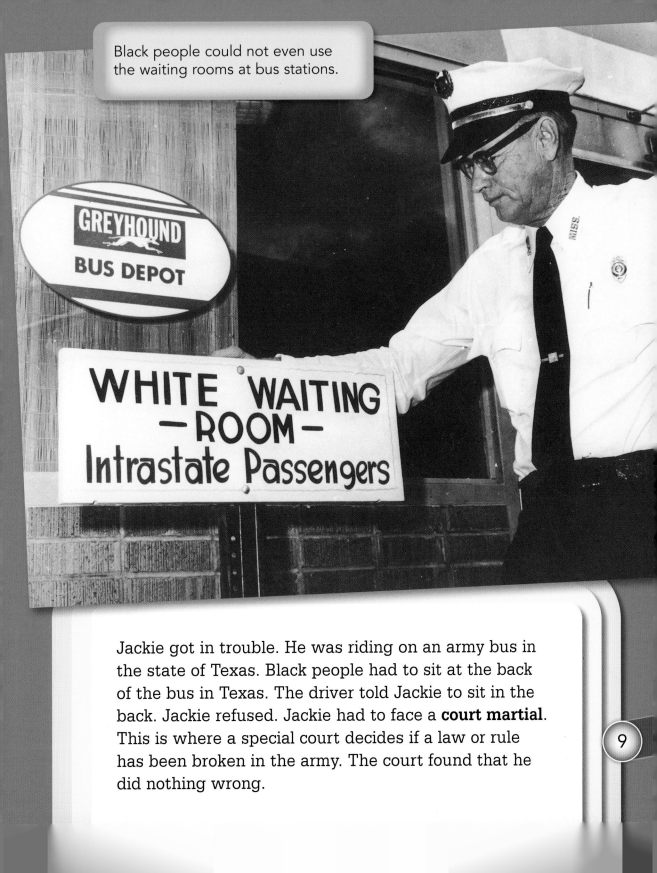

Black people could not even use the waiting rooms at bus stations.

GREYHOUND
BUS DEPOT

WHITE WAITING
—ROOM—
Intrastate Passengers

Jackie got in trouble. He was riding on an army bus in the state of Texas. Black people had to sit at the back of the bus in Texas. The driver told Jackie to sit in the back. Jackie refused. Jackie had to face a **court martial**. This is where a special court decides if a law or rule has been broken in the army. The court found that he did nothing wrong.

9

The Negro Leagues

Jackie left the army in 1944. He worked to be a **pro athlete**. Jackie signed up with a baseball team. The team was the Kansas City Monarchs. The Monarchs belonged to the **Negro Leagues**. *Negro* is a word that people used for blacks. The Negro Leagues were made up of black players.

Jackie wears his Kansas City Monarchs uniform.

Life in the Negro Leagues was hard. Baseball players travel a lot. They travel to play teams in different cities. But many restaurants would not serve black players. Hotels would not let them stay. Negro League players often ate and slept on a team bus.

The Negro Leagues were not part of Major League Baseball. They did not play Major League teams. They did not get as much attention. Therefore, Negro League players made less money. Many were very good. They could play in the Major Leagues. But no Major League team would take them.

Jackie only played for one year in the Negro Leagues.

Becoming a Dodger

Branch Rickey ran the Brooklyn Dodgers. It was a Major League baseball team in New York City. Rickey wanted black players on his team. He knew there were many good black athletes. Rickey wanted to help blacks. He also wanted to help the Dodgers win.

Major League teams had agreed to keep out black players. People had a name for this agreement. They called it "the **color barrier**." Rickey wanted to break the color barrier. But it would not be easy.

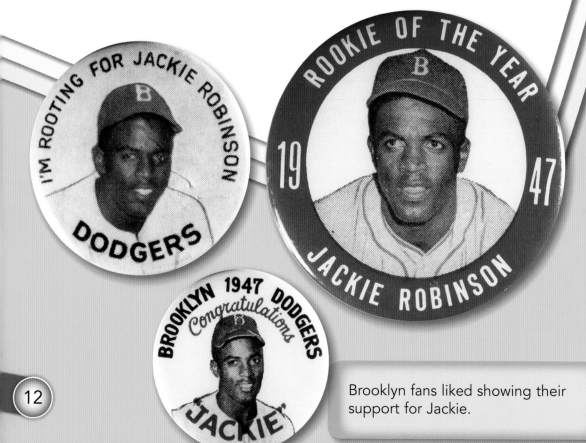

I'M ROOTING FOR JACKIE ROBINSON
DODGERS

ROOKIE OF THE YEAR
19 47
JACKIE ROBINSON

BROOKLYN 1947 DODGERS
Congratulations
JACKIE

Brooklyn fans liked showing their support for Jackie.

Branch Rickey (right) picked Jackie to break baseball's "color barrier."

Rickey needed a special black ballplayer. He would have to be good on the field. But he would also have to be tough.

Rickey chose Jackie Robinson. Rickey warned Jackie about what lay ahead. Jackie would have to ignore name-calling. He could not get angry. If he did, people would say blacks could not make it in the Major Leagues. Rickey warned that Jackie might even face violence. Jackie still agreed to do it.

Life in the Minor Leagues

Jackie signed on to play for the Brooklyn Dodgers. But he still had a lot to learn about baseball. Brooklyn sent him to a Minor League team. It was in Montreal. That is a city in Canada. Jackie would learn baseball skills there. He would learn how to play in the Major Leagues.

No black player had ever played in the Minor Leagues. So Jackie's first game was big news. The ballpark was full of fans. They wanted to see this special day. Jackie's first turn at bat did not go well. He hit a ground ball and was called out.

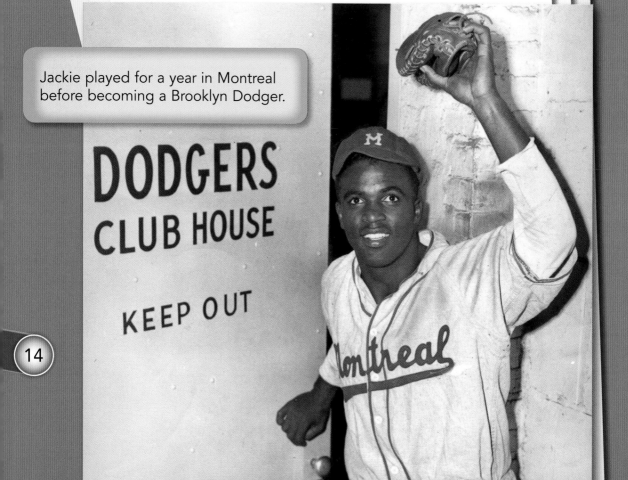

Jackie played for a year in Montreal before becoming a Brooklyn Dodger.

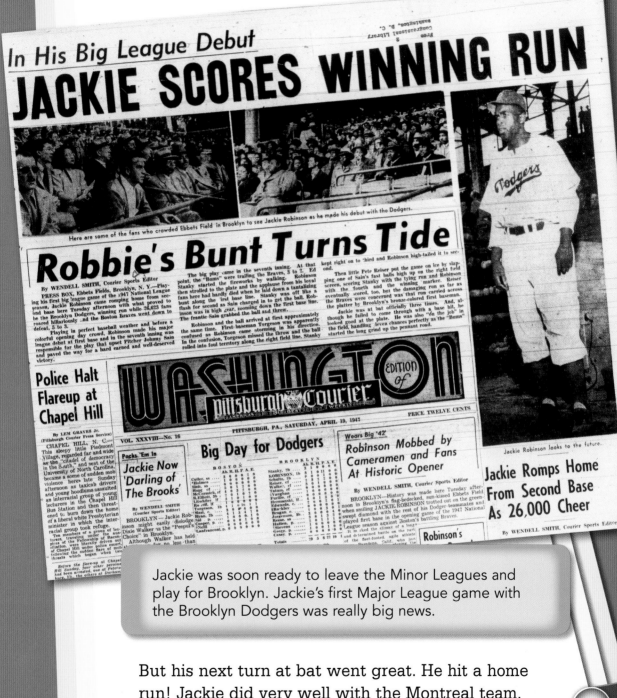

Jackie was soon ready to leave the Minor Leagues and play for Brooklyn. Jackie's first Major League game with the Brooklyn Dodgers was really big news.

But his next turn at bat went great. He hit a home run! Jackie did very well with the Montreal team. Montreal fans loved him. Outside Montreal was another story. Fans yelled names and booed him. So did opposing players. But at the end of the season, Jackie was ready to play for Brooklyn.

Pee Wee Reese is second in from the left. He helped Jackie become accepted as a Dodger.

"Did you see Jackie Robinson hit that ball?"

Becoming a Dodger was hard. White teammates did not want Jackie around at first.

Jackie played his first game as a Brooklyn Dodger on April 15, 1947. Fans packed the stadium. But Jackie played poorly his first week. At one game in Boston, fans yelled names at Jackie. One of Jackie's teammates was Pee Wee Reese. He decided to help Jackie. He put his arm around Jackie during a game. The whole crowd could see that Reese liked Jackie. The name-calling stopped.

Jackie started playing very well. He helped the Dodgers go to the World Series. That is the championship of baseball. The Dodgers lost the Series, but more people began cheering for Jackie. They even made up songs about him.

Death threats

Some people still did not want black players in the Major Leagues. They tried to scare Jackie out of playing. Letters like these threatened Jackie's life. They told him to never play in the city of Cincinnati. But nothing ever happened.

Most Valuable Player

Jackie did great his first year. In fact he won a special honor. He was named **Rookie** of the Year. A rookie is a beginner.

People wanted to see Jackie play. Ballparks set records for attendance when he played. One sports writer made up a poem about Jackie. He wrote "Jackie's nimble, Jackie's quick. Jackie's making the **turnstiles** click." Turnstiles are machines that count people going into ballparks.

Jackie continued to do well. In 1949, he was named his league's Most Valuable Player. That means he performed better than other players. Each year, his league chose an All-Star Team. Only the best players were named to it. Jackie made the All-Star Team six times.

Here Jackie holds one of his many awards.

rookie   player in the first year of the Major Leagues

JACKIE ROBINSON
"The Pride of Brooklyn"
as HIMSELF

THE JACKIE ROBINSON STORY

MINOR WATSON · RUBY DEE · RICHARD LANE

Directed by ALFRED E. GREEN who gave you "The Jolson Story"

Copyright 1950 Pathe Industries, Inc.

Jackie in Hollywood

Many people admired Jackie. In 1950, Hollywood made a movie about him. It was called "The Jackie Robinson Story." Jackie played himself in the starring role!

Winning the World Series

Jackie won many honors. But he still had not won the World Series. The Dodgers went to the Series four times between 1947 and 1954. Each time they lost to the New York Yankees.

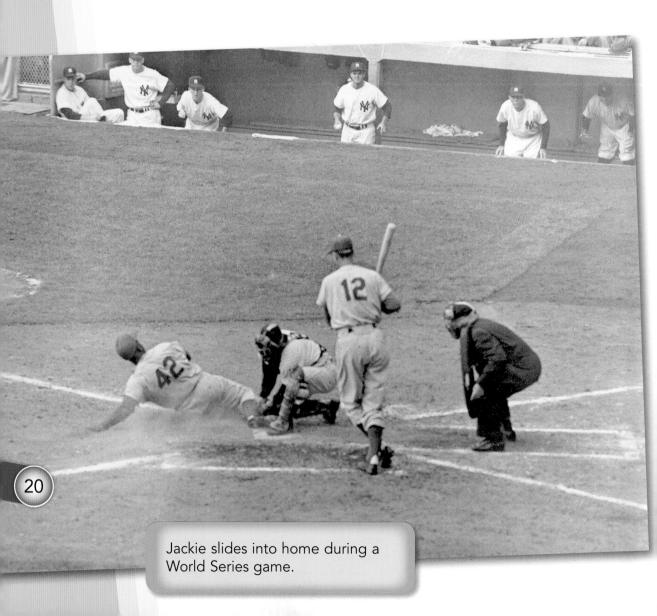

Jackie slides into home during a World Series game.

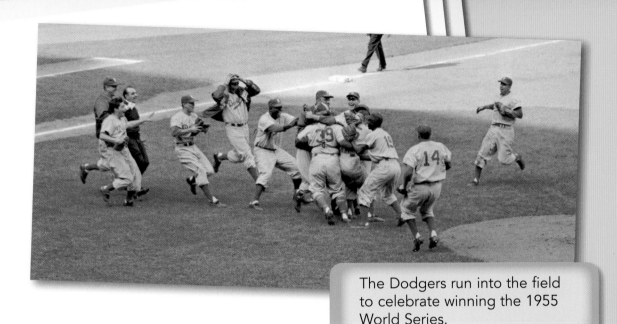

The Dodgers run into the field to celebrate winning the 1955 World Series.

Brooklyn fans joked about their team's losses. They called the Dodgers "Our Bums." But in 1955, the Dodgers got another chance. Once again, they played the Yankees. This time, they finally won! "It was one of the greatest thrills of my life," Jackie said.

But Jackie was getting old to be a ball player. He knew he would have to leave baseball soon. The 1956 season was his last.

Leaving Brooklyn

The Dodgers left Brooklyn after 1957. They moved to the city of Los Angeles in California. There were more fans in Los Angeles. That gave the owner more money. Brooklyn fans loved their "Bums." They were angry and upset to lose their team. They also lost Ebbets Field, the Dodger's stadium. It was torn down in 1960.

Life After Baseball

Jackie left baseball after the 1956 season. But he helped change the game. He broke the **color barrier**. After that, Major League teams began to hire black players. Jackie was a leader in **civil rights**. Civil rights are the freedoms all Americans are promised under U.S. laws. These include freedoms like the right to vote. Black people have had to fight hard for their civil rights. In 1956, Jackie won the Spingarn Medal. It honors civil rights champions.

Jackie and Rachel with David, Sharon, and Jackie Jr.

Jackie spoke out to get civil rights for all black Americans.

Jackie spoke out about problems faced by blacks. The Rev. Martin Luther King Jr. had also become a civil rights leader. Jackie worked with King to fight for civil rights. Black people had to fight hard for these rights.

Jackie's baseball job took him away from his family. Jackie and his wife, Rachel, raised three children. They had two sons and one daughter. Their names were Jackie Jr., Sharon, and David. After leaving baseball, Jackie wanted a job close to home. He went to work for a restaurant chain. The chain was called Chock Full O'Nuts. He held a top job. He helped make decisions and run the business.

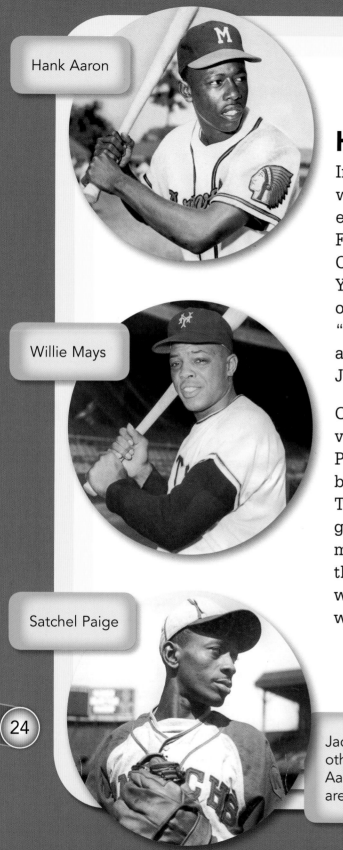

Hank Aaron

Willie Mays

Satchel Paige

Hall of Fame

In 1962, Jackie Robinson won a special award. He was elected to the Baseball Hall of Fame. The Hall of Fame is in Cooperstown, a city in New York. The Hall of Fame accepts only the best baseball players. "It's the greatest honor that any person can have," Jackie said.

Only certain people can be voted into the Hall of Fame. Players have to be out of baseball for at least five years. They must also have been a great player. It often takes many years to be elected to the Hall of Fame. But Jackie was elected the first year he was able to be chosen.

Jackie Robinson paved the way for other black baseball players. Hank Aaron, Willie Mays, and Satchel Paige are all in baseball's Hall of Fame.

Jackie made a speech when he won this award. He thanked his mother and his wife. He also thanked Branch Rickey. He said that Branch Rickey had been like a father to him. Winning the award gave him a sense of duty. "[I] must use it to help others," he said.

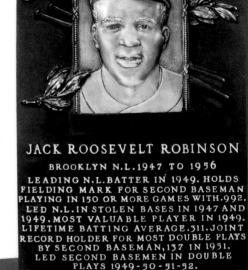

JACK ROOSEVELT ROBINSON
BROOKLYN N.L. 1947 TO 1956
LEADING N.L. BATTER IN 1949. HOLDS
FIELDING MARK FOR SECOND BASEMAN
PLAYING IN 150 OR MORE GAMES WITH .992.
LED N.L. IN STOLEN BASES IN 1947 AND
1949. MOST VALUABLE PLAYER IN 1949.
LIFETIME BATTING AVERAGE .311. JOINT
RECORD HOLDER FOR MOST DOUBLE PLAYS
BY SECOND BASEMAN, 137 IN 1951.
LED SECOND BASEMEN IN DOUBLE
PLAYS 1949-50-51-52.

Jackie becomes part of the Baseball Hall of Fame. He stands with Branch Rickey, his wife, Rachel, and his mother.

"I Never Had It Made"

Jackie wrote a book about his life. It was called *I Never Had It Made*. He wrote about his days as a Dodger. He wrote about pitchers who tried to hurt him. They threw balls right at him. Other players slid into him and hit him with the spikes on their shoes. But Jackie also wrote about good things that happened to him. He wrote about people who helped. He wrote about Branch Rickey and Pee Wee Reese. He wrote about his family.

Robinson wrote another book, too. This one was called *Baseball Has Done It*. It was about players who broke the **color barrier** in Major League Baseball.

Many people looked up to Jackie Robinson. He accomplished a lot in his life.

In 1972, Jackie appeared in public for one of the last times. He went to Dodger Stadium in Los Angeles. The Dodgers honored Jackie. They marked the 25th anniversary of his first season in Major League Baseball.

Jackie was not young any more. He had white hair and moved slowly. In fact, Jackie was sick. He would die on October 24, 1972, from a heart attack. Jackie Robinson was only 53 years old.

Number 42

Baseball players have numbers on their uniforms. Jackie's number was 42. Many teams **retire** a player's number. *Retire* means they stop using it after he leaves the game. It is a sign of respect. It means that nobody can take the place of that player.

In 1972, the Dodgers retired Jackie's number. Old teammates remembered him. One was Duke Snider. Snider is in the Baseball Hall of Fame, too. "[Jackie] was the greatest competitor I have ever seen," Snider said.

Major League teams have honored Jackie by retiring number 42.

In 1997, Major League teams honored Jackie in a new way. It had been 50 years since Jackie's first game. So each baseball team retired Robinson's No. 42. Now, no other Major League player can wear No. 42.

On special days that rule is reversed. In 2007, baseball players held a Jackie Robinson Day. One player from each team wore No. 42. In some cases, the whole team wore No. 42. Jackie's memory lives on.

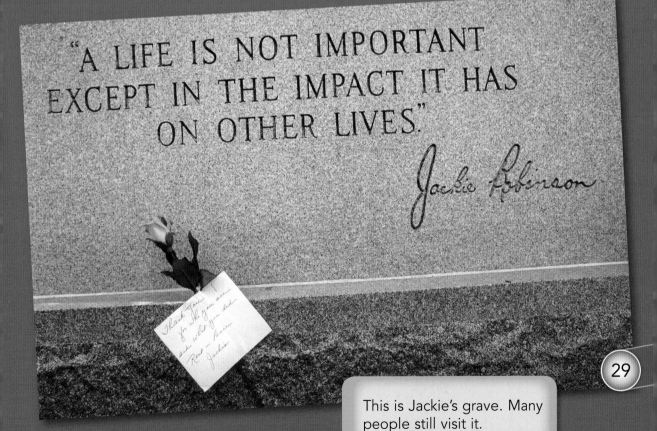

"A LIFE IS NOT IMPORTANT EXCEPT IN THE IMPACT IT HAS ON OTHER LIVES."

Jackie Robinson

This is Jackie's grave. Many people still visit it.

Glossary

civil rights freedoms all Americans are promised under U.S. laws

color barrier agreement by baseball teams to not hire black players

court martial special court used just by the army

draft require people to join the army

Jim Crow laws laws that separated whites and blacks

officer person in the army who leads others

pro athlete someone who is paid to play sports

retire stop using something

rookie player in the first year of the Major Leagues. A beginner.

segregate separate blacks and whites

turnstile machine that counts people going into ballparks

Want to Know More?

Books to read

Christopher, Matt and Glenn Stout. *Jackie Robinson: Legends in Sports.* New York: Little, Brown, 2006

Denenberg, Barry. *Stealing Home: The Jackie Robinson Story.* New York: Scholastic, 1990.

Websites

http://www.jackierobinson.com/home.html
Visit Jackie Robinson's official website to learn more about his life and amazing career.

http://www.time.com/time/time100/heroes/profile/robinson01.html
Read a tribute to Jackie Robinson written by home run slugger Henry Aaron.

Places to visit

National Baseball Hall of Fame
25 Main Street • Cooperstown, New York 13326 • Call 1-888-HALL-OF-FAME
http://web.baseballhalloffame.org/visit/
Go find out more about Jackie and other great baseball players.

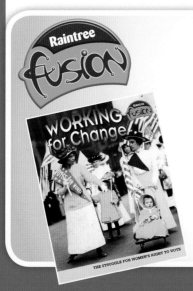

Read *When Will I Get In?: Segregation and Civil Rights* to find out about the struggle against segregation.

Read *Working for Change: The Struggle for Women's Right to Vote* to find out about the long fight for women's voting rights.

Index